Cycling in Nottinghamshire

ARNOLD ROBINSON

© 1990

ISBN 0 946404 17 8

Printed and Published by
J. H. Hall & Sons Limited, Siddals Road, Derby
Printers and Stationers since 1831
Telephone: Derby (0332) 45218
Fax: (0332) 296146

Cover design: Richard Jones, Hall - Derby

THE NOTTINGHAMSHIRE HERITAGE SERIES

Contents

Map showing location of cycling routes

An Introduction to 'Cycling in Nottinghamshire'
Key to Route Maps / Itineraries

Cycling Routes	**Miles**
Rides from Nottingham	
1 The Southern Tip	35½
2 The Vale of Belvoir	28½
3 Newstead Abbey & Hoveringham	32¾
Rides from Mansfield	
4 Oxton and Newstead	33½
5 Sherwood Forest	25¼
Rides from Worksop	
6 Carburton & Clumber	21½
7 Carlton-in-Lindrick & Blyth	32¾
Rides from East Retford	
8 Wiseton, Littleborough & Laneham	37¼
9 Bothamsall, Tuxford & Laxton	31¼
Rides from Newark-upon-Trent	
10 Southwell, Oxton & Fiskerton	30
11 Kirklington & Laxton	35½
12 Staunton-in-the-Vale & Aslockton	30

Bibliography

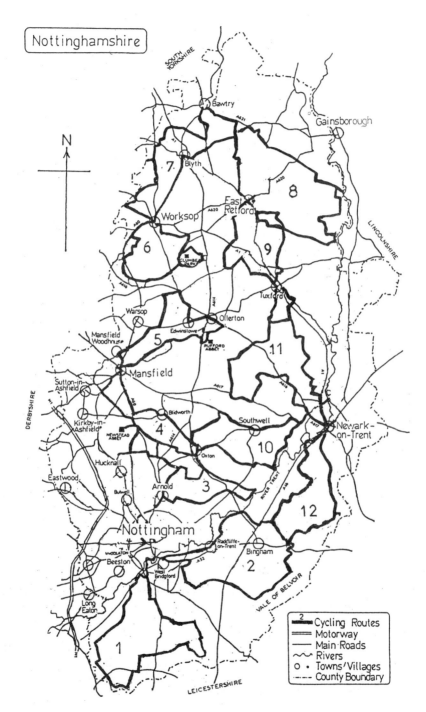

An Introduction to
CYCLING IN NOTTINGHAMSHIRE

Nottinghamshire has long been associated with cycling and cyclists. For almost a century, cycles have been built here although some names like Humber and Fletcher are now just a memory. Others such as Raleigh and Carlton whose names are known throughout the world, still continue even though their image has changed from the thirties and the immediate post war years when cycling was at its peak. In more recent times new names such as Columbia and Aende are building bikes for the connoisseur.

In the county are numerous well known and very active cycling clubs whose members have made some memorable rides in time trials held along the A1 and other main roads.

At the same time, touring cyclists, many of them members of the Cyclists' Touring Club, explore the quiet little used byways which criss-cross the county and provide excellent cycling routes for leisure riding away from the heavy traffic which now roars along the main roads.

The Cycling Routes

Many of the routes described in this guide are based upon my earliest cycle rides when I was resident in Mansfield in the thirties. I rode over them recently and found them little changed. Only in a few cases has a byroad been closed or diverted.

Gone are the days when it was quite reasonable to ride two abreast along the Fosse Way but some ancient highways from the stage coach days now make ideal cycling routes, eg the Old Great North Road to the Jockey House *(Ride No. 9)*. There are also some excellent off highway routes in Sherwood Forest and the Dukeries, always a favourite cycling area.

In recent years, 'new' objectives for rides include Clumber Park to which cyclists are admitted without charge and where there is a Cycle Hire Centre *(Rides Nos. 5 and 6)*.

Although each of the rides has been arranged in the form of a circuit suitable for a day ride, several of the rides might easily be combined to form a longer tour. By using the suggested routes as a framework, a number of exended circuits could be devised.

The gradients of all the routes are relatively *easy*. There are few steep hills but for beginners or others who do not feel able to ride the distance suggested, alternative shorter rides are indicated on the route maps and in the itineraries. Most of the suggested routes could in fact be divided into two or even three shorter rides.

Maps

The route maps are sufficiently detailed within the scope of the scale to enable a rider to follow the itinerary but greater detail will be found on the Ordnance Survey Landranger maps, Sheets 111, 120, 121, 129 and 130.

Key to Route Maps

——————	Cycling Routes
▬ ▬ ▬ ▬	Alternative Cycling Routes
──────	Other Roads
• • • • • • • •	Unsurfaced Roads
++++++++	Railways
~~	Rivers/Streams
〰〰	Lakes/Reservoirs
░░░░	Built up areas
○ ○	Towns/Villages
+	Church
⋊	Camp Site
■ •	Places of interest
—·—·—··	County Boundary

Key to abbreviations in Itineraries

EC   Early Closing Day
MD   Market Day
Inf   Tourist Information Office
BR   British Rail Station
B&B   Bed and Breakfast in vicinity
Cmg   Camping Site in vicinity
PM   Pub Meals   ⎫ There may be limited
C   Cafe or Restaurant ⎬ opening hours/days
Sh   Shop(s)   ⎭
Cyc   Cycle Repairer
CH   Cycle Hire
NT   National Trust Property
T   Toilets
P   Picturesque road, place or area
TL   Traffic Lights
TR   Traffic Roundabout
Sp   Signpost

Ride No. 1 THE SOUTHERN TIP 35¾ miles / 57.0 kms

Start: Nottingham (Wilford Bridge)

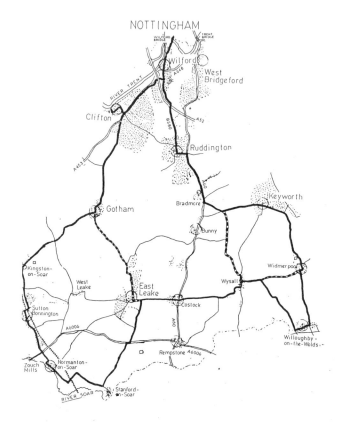

After leaving the suburbs of Nottingham, the whole of this ride is along quiet rural byways in the southern tip of the county.

Gradients: Very gentle with few hills and none of any severity.

Miles	Places, Information and Itinerary	Points of Interest and scenic attractions
	NOTTINGHAM. *EC: Thurs. MD: Wed., Sat. BR. Inf. B&B., Sh. C. Cyc.*	Busy industrial city with many places of interest eg. Castle, c.1068; now Museum and Art Gallery, ancient inns, Goose Fair, Wollaton Hall - cycle museum.

	Wilford Bridge Cross bridge and continue into:	Former toll bridge, use now restricted to pedestrians and cyclists.
¾	**Wilford.** *SH.* Cont ahead to × rds (TL); cont str ahead and in ½m turn R (Launceston Cres) cont to subway and follow cycle signs; cross A453 (care needed), and cont on cycleway; turn R into:	Small suburb which still retains its village atmosphere. Cycling route avoids a busy road junction and crossing.
3	**Clifton** (Village) *Sh.* Cont to church then retrace route and at junc A453, turn R; in ¼m at TR fork L on u/c byroad, cont to:	Picturesque village now almost surrounded by large housing estate; Hall, 18c; church, Clifton Grove, tree lined walk above River Trent. In the 30's, its cottage tea rooms were popular with cyclists.
3½	**Gotham.** *Sh.* Turn R (sp Kingston-on-Soar), fork R (see note a); in 1½m at × rds, cont ahead to:	Rather forlorn village, know for the legend about the Wise Men of Gotham who built a hedge around a cuckoo; church, 13c-14c.
2¾	**Kingston-on-Soar.** Turn L (sp Sutton Bonnington), cont ahead to:	Hall, estate village; church, Babington Chantrey.
2	**Sutton Bonnington.** *Sh.* Cont to T junc (A6006), turn R to:	Formerly two villages each with its own church, old houses, University of Nottingham Agricultural College.
1¼	**Zouch Mills.** Retrace route and in ¼m turn R (sp Normanton) cont to:	River Soar.
1	**Normanton-on-Soar.** Cont ahead to outskirts of Stanford-on-Soar, turn L, cont past Stanford Hall to T junc (A6006), turn R and in 150 yds turn L, (sp East Leake); at × rds cont str ahead to outskirts of:	Plough Inn, Church, views of hills of Charnwood Forest and Soar Valley.

4¾	**East Leake.** *EC: Wed. Sh. PM.* At T junc, turn R and cont to:	Formerly small village now extended by housing development; church, shawn (trumpet).
1¼	**Costock.** Cross over A60 and cont on byroad to:	Small village on busy A60 Nottingham-Loughborough road.
2¼	**Wysall.** Turn L at church and in 200 yds, then turn R (sp Willoughby) (see note b); in ½m turn R (sp Willoughby), cont through open country and in 1½m turn L into:	Attractive village; church, pulpit, screen.
2½	**Willoughby-on-the-Wolds.** Turn L to:	Church.
2	**Widmerpool.** Turn R and in 200 yds turn L, in ¼m climb hill and cont to outskirts of:	Picturesque village.
2½	**Keyworth.** *EC: Wed. Sh.* Bear L through village, and in 1½m at × rds turn R; in ½m at T junc (A60) turn R through:	Church - 15c. tower/spire.
1¾	**Bradmore.** Cont ahead on A60 (busy road) for 1¼m, at × rds (TL) turn L (B680) into:	Ruins of Church, only tower/spire remains after fire in 1706.
1½	**Ruddington.** *Sh.* At × rds in centre of village, turn R (B680); cont ahead passing under A52 to:	Framework Museum, formerly small village now developed.
2	**Wilford.** *Sh.* At × rds (TL) str ahead thro village to:	
¾	**Wilford Bridge.**	

Notes
(a) From Gotham, there is a direct route to East Leake (see map).
(b) From Wysall, there is a direct route to Bradmore (see map).

Ride No. 2   THE VALE OF BELVOIR   30 Miles / 48.0 kms

Start: Nottingham (Trent Bridge)

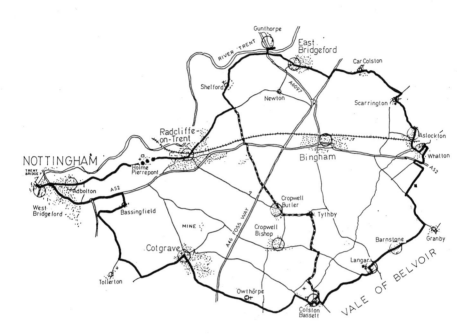

There is a wide choice of quiet byroads between the City of Nottingham and the Vale of Belvoir which the county shares with Leicestershire. This ride includes some of the best and most interesting rides in this area.

Gradients: Very gentle throughout with just one short climb into East Bridgeford.

Miles	Places, Information and Itinerary	Points of interest and scenic attractions
	NOTTINGHAM. *EC: Thurs. MD: Wed., Sat. BR. Inf. B&B., Sh. C. Cyc.*	Busy industrial city with many places of interest eg. Castle, c.1068; now Museum and Art Gallery, ancient inns, Goose Fair, Wollaton Hall - cycle museum.

▲ The cross at Colston Bassett, a peaceful village in the south of the county, is in the care of the National Trust. The nearby shelter makes an ideal place for a picnic

◀ Cyclists stop to study the pile of discarded horseshoes outside the Smithy at Scarrington.

	Trent Bridge. After crossing bridge, turn L (sp A52 Grantham) and in ½m fork L on u/c road, cont through:	An impressive bridge across River Trent; Nottm Forest FC ground on L; Trent Bridge cricket ground on R.
1	**Adbolton.** Cont str ahead and at T junc, turn L past entrance to Country Park; cont ahead on 'Private Road' (unsurfaced, gated) through:	National Water Sports Centre on L.
2	**Holme Pierrepont.** Cont to T junc, turn L into:	Church - monuments. Hall.
1½	**Radcliffe-on-Trent.** EC: Wed, Sh, T. In centre of village, turn L on byroad, in 1½m at × rds, turn L (see note a); desc steeply into:	Formerly small village now extended by housing development.
1¾	**Shelford.** Cont ahead for 1½m and at × rds (A6097) turn L across Gunthorpe Bridge, and imm turn R into:	Lane to Stoke Bardolph Ferry.
1½	**Gunthorpe.** PM. T. Retrace route across bridge and at × rds, turn L on narrow byroad; climb steeply into:	River Trent, attractive river side, usually very busy on summer weekends. Cuttle Hill.
1	**East Bridgeford.** EC: Wed. PM. C. Sh. At × rds cont str ahead to T junc (A46 - Fosse Road, busy trunk road); turn L and in ¼m turn R (extreme care neccessary) into narrow byroad to:	Church on Saxon site. Site of Roman Station of Margidunum.
1¾	**Car Colston.** Fork R and cont to T junc, turn R into:	Peaceful village with large green and cricket field. Church - 14c, chancel; Hall - 17c.
1¾	**Scarrington.** Turn L (sp Aslockton); cont for 1m to T junc and turn R into:	Discarded horse shoes piled at side of smithy; Peaceful village.
1	**Aslockton.** Cross level × g and in 200 yds turn L through:	River Smite; village assoc with Archbishop Cranmer.

½	**Whatton.** Cont to T junc (A52); turn R (care needed) and in 150 yds, turn L into byroad; turn L then R and cont to T junc, turn R and in 1m on approach to Granby, turn R; cont thro:	Diversion around backroads of village recommended; picturesque cottages.
3½	**Barnstone** To:	Views of Belvoir Castle and wooded hills to south east.
1	**Langar.** EC: Wed. C. At × rds, cont str ahead into village; turn L and at T junc turn R; in ¼m turn L on field road; cont for 1½m and at T junc, turn R; in 150 yds turn L into narrow road, then turn R then L into:	Church - impressive tower; Howe monuments; cottages; Unicorn Inn. Pleasant village. Has historical associations but there is now little to see. Nearby airfield used for parachuting.
2	**Colston Bassett.** Turn R at cross and in ½m turn L; in 1m at × rds cont str ahead through:	Picturesque village; Cross - National Trust. Old Church in ruins in park; Hall. River Smite.
2	**Owthorpe.** Climb for ½m then cont to × rds (A46, Fosse Road). Cont str ahead, (Care neccessary), desc steep hill and cont to:	Former Grantham Canal crossed. Church.
2	**Cotgrave.** Sh. At church, turn L and in 1¼m turn R, in ¾m at T junc turn R; cont past Airport to:	Modern colliery to north of village.
4¼	**Bassingfield.** C. Turn L to T junc (A52 - dual carriageway) and turn L (busy road); at TR cont str ahead through outskirts of West Bridgeford to:	Quiet village near to the busy A52 Nottingham-Grantham road.
1¾	**TRENT BRIDGE**	

Notes

(a) From the × rds, ¾m before Shelford, a turn to the R is a direct route to Colston Bassett (see map).

Ride No. 3 NEWSTEAD ABBEY and HOVERINGHAM   34¾ miles / 55.5 kms

Start: Daybrook

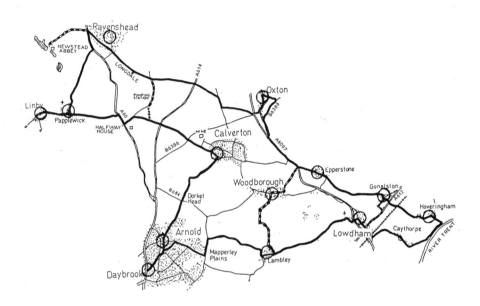

This ride links together Newstead Abbey and Trentside at Hoveringham and passes through several quiet peaceful villages in the heart of the county.

Gradients: Although there are more hills than on the first two rides, none of them are very steep.

Miles	Places, Information and Itinerary	Points of interest and scenic attractions
	DAYBROOK. *Sh. C.* At TL turn R (sp Arnold); Cont into:	Bustling suburb on A60 Mansfield Road.
¾	**Arnold.** *Sh.* Turn L (Hallams Lane), turn L (Derby St), again turn L then R past church; climb to:	Busy suburb.

13

The frontage of the old smithy at Gonalston is built in the form of a horseshoe.

1½	**Dorket Head.** At × rds cont str ahead then desc steeply to:	Open country with extensive views.
1¾	**Calverton.** *EC: Wed, Sh. C.* At × rds, turn L and climb to × rds (junc B6386); cont str ahead and climb to:	Birthplace of stocking frame, the former country village now extended since colliery was opened.
2¼	**Junc A614** (Nottingham-Ollerton road). Cont str ahead and (see note a) desc to:	Care reqd as view restricted. Burntstump Country Park on L.
1¼	**Halfway House.** C. Junc A60. Turn R and in ¼m turn L (B6011) cont to:	
1½	**Papplewick.** At × rds cont str ahead to:	Hall, Church, Mill, River Leen.
1	**Linby.** Retrace route to × rds at:	Crosses, Old Houses, Picturesque, Church.
1	**Papplewick.** Turn L through village; climb for ½m then cont to T junc (A60), turn L to:	Hall, Church, Mill, River Leen.
2¼	**Ravenshead.** Turn R opp gates into byroad and desc to:	Gates to Newstead Abbey on L; Visit recommended, once home of Lord Byron; attractive grounds.
1½	**Longdale.** C. At × rds cont str ahead; in 1m at × rds (A614 - busy road), cont str ahead; at T junc turn R and in ¼m turn L, cont to TR (A6097) and cont str ahead into:	Picturesque road through forest. Papplewick Pumping Station down lane on R.
4	**OXTON.** *EC: Wed, Sh. PM.* Turn R and in ½m at T junc, turn R (B6386), in ½m at T junc turn L on byroad; in ½m turn L on A6097 (busy road); in 1m turn L to (see note b):	Parkland setting; Church: citation for VC awarded to Capt (later Rear Admiral) R St. V. Sherbrooke, commander of HMS Onslow at battle of North Cape, December 1944.
3	**Epperstone.** *PM.* Cont thro village and fork L on byroad to:	

1¾	**Gonalston.** Turn L (see note c) and at × rds (A612) cont str ahead on byroad to:	Old Smithy, entrance.
1½	**HOVERINGHAM.** *PM. C.* Fork R and cont alongside River Trent to:	Site of former ferry across River Trent. Cafe is popular cyclists rendezvous.
1½	**Caythorpe.** Cont to T junc and turn R over level × g into:	Small hamlet.
1¼	**LOWDHAM.** *EC: Wed. Sh.* At × rds, cont along main street and in ¼m, turn L into byroad; at × rds (junc A6097) cont str ahead and cont to:	Church, 12-13c, font. Main street was formerly the main road.
2¾	**Lambley.** *Sh. C.* At far end of village, bear L; climb steeply then cont ahead for 1½m to T junc (B684), turn L to:	Church. Small village in valley.
2½	**Mapperley Plains.** *Sh.* In ½m turn R thro residential area and desc to:	
1½	**DAYBROOK**	

Notes

This ride may be shortened if required by:

(a) After crossing A614, turning R on unsurfaced road and riding direct to Longdale (see map). This omits Papplewick, Linby and Newstead.

(b) Turning R (sp Woodborough) and riding direct to Lambley via Woodborough (see map). This omits diversion to Hoveringham and Lowdham.

(c) Turning R in Gonalston and riding along A612 direct to Lowdham (see map). This omits diversion to Hoveringham.

Ride No. 4   OXTON, NEWSTEAD   26½ miles / 42.5 kms
and TEVERSAL

Start: Mansfield (Titchfield Park, Nottingham Road)

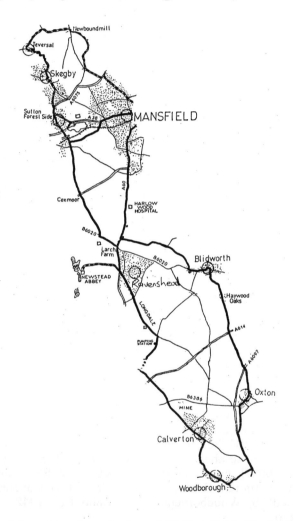

The first part of this ride is along the busy A60 Mansfield - Nottingham Road but then much of it is on quiet byways, first to Blidworth and Oxton and returning through the Longdale Valley to Newstead Abbey. For the more energetic, there is then an optional extension of the ride to Skegby and Teversal although this involves first riding through a built-up area around Sutton-in-Ashfield.

Gradients: Variable with a few relatively easy climbs and descents.

Miles	Places, Information and Itinerary	Points of interest and scenic attractions
	MANSFIELD. *EC: Wed, MD: Tues, Thurs, Sat. Sh. C. T. Cyc.* Follow Nottingham Road (A60) out of town, climbing steadily for 1m then desc for ¾m, again climb to:	Ancient Market town, the centre of which is largely pedestrianized. Although surrounded by collieries, there is also much rural and wooded scenery; River Maun, Bentinck Memorial in Market Place. Rock Houses.
2½	**Harlow Wood Hospital.** Desc for ½m then climb for ¼m and at × rds (no sp), turn L on undulating byroad and cont for 2m to:	A famous Orthopaedic Hospital in a woodland setting. Sheppard's Stone on L at foot of hill at scene of murder. Table Top Tree at corner. Views of Fountain Dale on L.
3½	**Blidworth.** *Sh.* Turn L and desc thro village, at foot of hill, turn R (Dale Rd) and imm turn R (Haywood Oaks Lane) climb for ¼m then desc thro:	Ancient custom of 'Rocking Ceremony' in church on 2nd February.
1¼	**Haywood Oaks.** Cont desc through forest to × rds (A614, busy road); cont str ahead (sp Golf Club); in 1m at × rds (A6097 - dual carriageway), cont str ahead (sp Oxton) on byroad and desc to:	Small farming hamlet. Ancient oaks in vicinity. Oxton Golf Club on R in beautiful setting.
3	**OXTON.** *EC: Wed, PM. Sh.* Cont thro village and at Bridge Inn, turn L (B6386); when this turns L cont str ahead; at T junc (A6097), turn L (busy road); in 1m turn R (care needed) (Sp Woodborough); cont to:	Parkland setting. Church: Citation for VC awarded to Capt (later Rear Admiral) R St. V. Sherbrooke; VC, DSP, RN. commander of HMS Onslow at battle of North Cape, Dec. 1942.
3¼	**WOODBOROUGH.** *Sh.* Turn R along main street and at far end, turn R (sp Calverton); climb for ½m then desc steeply to T junc, turn L through:	Large village in valley. Conservation area. Church, St. Swithens.

1½	**Calverton.** *EC: Wed. Sh. C.* Cont along Main Street and in 1m at × rds (B6386), cont str ahead (C on left); in ¾m at × rds (junc (A614), cont str ahead (care needed, view restricted; in ¼m imm before LH bend, turn R on unsurfaced road, desc for ½m then cont on surfaced byroad, at × rds turn L to:	Birthplace of stocking frame. Former small country village now extended since colliery was sunk. Papplewick Pumping Station on L, occ open to public.
4¼	**Longdale.** *C.* Cont ahead to T junc (A60) at:	Picturesque valley road through forest.
1½	**Ravenshead.** Turn R for ½m to Larch Farm × rds (TL), turn L (B6020) (see note a); and in ½m turn R on byroad; cont to × rds (A611) at:	Gates to Newstead Abbey opposite, once home of Lord Byron, attractive grounds. Visit recommended.
2½	**Coxmoor Cross Roads.** Cont str ahead and after short climb desc to × rds (TL), cont ahead and in 150 yds turn R (Hamilton Road) (see note b); cont ahead on Hermitage Lane and climb to T junc (A38); turn R and at TL cont str ahead; desc into:	Open country with views. Coxmoor Golf Club on R.
3½	**MANSFIELD**	

Notes
(a) For a direct route back to Mansfield, cont str ahead on A60 (see map).
(b) For the extension of the ride to Skegby and Teversal:
Additional distance 4¼ miles.

Cont str ahead across level × g; at × rds (TL) cont ahead to:

¾	**Sutton (Forest Side).** *EC: Wed, MD: Fri, Sat. Sh. C.* At junc A38, turn L and imm turn R (sp Skegby); cont to T junc, turn R and imm fork L to:	The route passes to the east of the town centre.

¾	**Skegby.** At T junc, turn L (B6014), desc for ¼m then turn R (Buttery Lane) into byroad, climb steeply and in ¼m turn R on narrow winding byroad, cont to:	Straggling village on Mansfield - Tibshelf road.
1¼	**Teversal.** Turn R (sp Pleasley) and cont on byroad, at T junc turn R then desc to:	Church, 12c doorway; Molyneux pew, c1684.
1¾	**Newboundmill.** At × rds turn R and in 100 yds turn L, at next junc bear R then cont to Penniment Farms; fork L to T junc (A6075): turn L and in 100 yds turn R (Westfield Lane) (busy road, care needed), cont into:	River Meden.
3½	**MANSFIELD**	

Newstead Abbey and its beautiful grounds, can be visited on either Ride 3 (from Nottingham) or Ride 4 (from Mansfield)

Ride No. 5   SHERWOOD FOREST   25¼ miles / 40.5 kms

Start: Mansfield (Leeming Street)

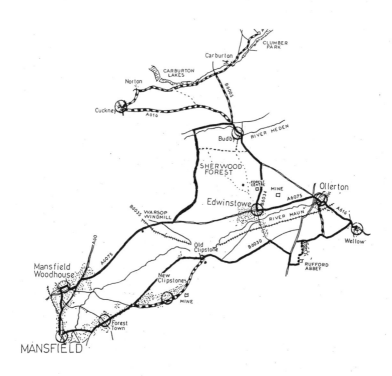

Sherwood Forest, famous for its association with the legend of Robin Hood, is without doubt the most attractive area of Nottinghamshire and it offers some excellent cycling routes, many of them on forest drives. This comparitively short ride provides an opportunity to see the best of the Forest.

Gradients: Very easy with no hills of any consequence.

Miles	Places, Information and Itinerary	Points of interest and scenic attractions
	MANSFIELD. EC: Wed, MD: Tues, Thurs, Sat. Sh. C. T. Cyc. Take A60 N; in ¾m pass under rly bridge and then take **2nd** turn L; cont ahead and desc to × rds, cont ahead into:	Ancient Market town, the centre of which is largely pedestrianized. Although surrounded by collieries, there is also much rural and wooded scenery; River Maun, Bentinck Memorial in Market Place. Rock Houses.

A pleasant approach to Rufford Abbey Country Park is by the footpath which runs from the Saw Mill alongside the Lake.

1¼	**Mansfield Woodhouse.** *EC: Thurs.* Sh. At T junc turn R along main street, in ¼m fork R and in 200 yds at TL turn L; at junc with A60, turn L and in ¼m turn R (Peafield Lane); climb easily and cont into open country to:	Ordinary village now virtually a suburb of Mansfield. Church - 14c tower and spire. Parliament Oak on R (in 3m).
3½	**Warsop Windmill** (× rds). Cont ahead and in ¼m turn L through gate on forest drive; cont ahead (see note a) for 2¾m to gate; turn R on byroad; cont to × rds and turn R (see note b), in 100 yds at T junc turn R (A616) into:	Windmill now disused. Pict drive (reasonable surface).
4	**Budby.** C Cont on A616 for 1m then turn R (sp B6034 Edwinstowe); climb easily for ¾m to:	Mobile Snack Bar off A616. Small hamlet in pict location in Sherwood Forest. Victorian Letter Box in village.
1¾	**Forest Visitors Centre** (on R) C. Cont on B6034 into:	Visit rec. Exhibition depicting Forest Life; Shop, walk to Major Oak tree also recommended.
½	**Edwinstowe.** Sh. C. At × rds, turn L (A6075), cont for 1½m to TR; take 4th exit (road closed to motor traffic) into:	Church: 13c according to legend, Robin Hood and Maid Marian were married here; former forest village spoiled by nearby coal mine. River Maun.
1¾	**Ollerton.** *EC: Thurs.* Sh. cont ahead through village (see note c) and climb easily to T junc; turn R (A616) and cont ahead and at × rds cont str ahead into:	River Maun. Pict village. Hop Pole Inn, formerly a coaching inn.
1¼	**Wellow.** PM. Sh. Retrace route to × rds and turn L on byroad; cont for 1¼m and then desc to Ford (footbridge available); imm turn L through Car Park adj Saw Mill; walk along path on either side of Rufford Lake into:	Pleasant village which has had little modernisation. Green, Maypole. Maypole Ceremony on Spring Bank Holiday.

2¾	**Rufford Abbey Country Park.** C. Craft Shop. Cont through Car Park and along drive to main gate; turn R along A614 (busy road, care needed); in 200 yds turn L (sp Edwinstowe and in ¾m at × rds (TL), turn L (B6030 Mansfield); cont to:	Abbey now in ruins, was formerly seat of Savilles who left in 1939; Estate suffered from war-time occupation. It became a Country Park in 1969 and parts of gardens have been reclaimed. Note gates on R.
3½	**Old Clipstone.** Fork R on byroad (see note d) and in 100 yds cont str ahead on farm drive cont to Cavendish Lodge, keep to L on drive and cont to gate (junc B6030); cont str ahead thro:	Ruins of King John's Palace, 13c. in field on L. Drive is surfaced but in poor condition.
3½	**Forest Town.** Sh. Cont str ahead and in ¾m turn R, desc for ½m then climb into:	Colliery village.
1½	**MANSFIELD**	

Notes

(a) A forest drive on the R (sp Bridleway) leads direct to Budby (see map).

(b) The ride might be extended to include Carburton Lakes and/or Clumber Park; an additional 11 miles. (See Map).

(c) The narrow byroad on the right. 200 yds beyond centre of Ollerton village, is a direct route to Rufford Country Park (see map).

(d) From Old Clipstone, there is an alternative route along the B6030 via New Clipstone (see map).

Ride No. 6   **CARBURTON and**   21¾ miles / 34.5 kms
                   CLUMBER

Start: Worksop (Newcastle Avenue, St. Anns' Church)

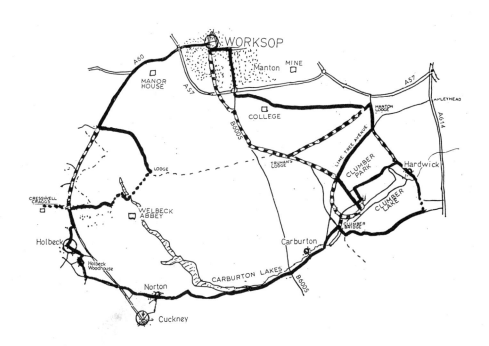

Although this ride starts along a busy main road, it soon provides an opportunity to explore some peaceful bridleways and byroads away from motor traffic and to visit two of the highlights of The Dukeries: Carburton Lakes and Clumber Park.

Gradients: Very easy with no steep hills.

Miles	Places, Information and Itinerary	Points of interest and scenic attractions
	WORKSOP. *EC: Thurs, MD: Sat. BR. Sh. C. Cyc.* Cont along Newcastle Av to TR (Ring Road); cont ahead on A60 and fork L (sp Mansfield); in 1m at × rds, turn L on byroad (see note a); cont to:	Priory Gatehouse, 14 cent.; Church - Norman; busy town, centre of coal mining area but nevertheless is the 'Gateway to The Dukeries.' River Ryton. Chesterfield Canal.

On a winter ride, cyclists leave the church at Carburton and turn towards Clumber Park, one of the most delightful parts of Nottinghamshire.

3	**Lodge.** Imm after lodge, turn R through trees then again turn R (sp Bridleway); at 2nd gate turn L along field track, cont to T junc and turn R then fork R and in further 100 yds, turn L on another field track passing rugby pitches of Welbeck College; cont to T junc and turn R on concrete road through field; in ¼m fork L and cont on drive to × rds at:	On R, was once the start of the Welbeck Tunnel (now closed). Track is grassy but rutted, it can be ridden with care. This is a peaceful cycling route away from traffic.
1¾	**Junc A60.** Turn L (Cafe and Cycle Dealer in Garden Centre on L); in ½m turn R to:	The drive opp leads to Cresswell Craggs Visitors Centre (in Derbyshire). Cafe is popular cyclists' rendezvous.
1	**Holbeck.** *B&B.* At foot of hill, turn L on drive past church; at × rds, turn R then fork L on narrow byroad; in ¼m at × rds turn L and cont to × rds (junc A60); cont str ahead to:	Members of Portland family are buried in churchyard.
1¾	**Norton.** *B&B. Sh.* At T junc turn L and imm turn R; in ¼m turn R and cont alongside Carburton Lakes; cont to × rds (C on R).	On L, Memorial to Lord George Bentinck. This is one of the finest cycle rides in Nottinghamshire. Wild Life.
2¾	**Carburton.** Cont str ahead through gateway at start of Lime Tree Avenue, cross br (River Poulter) and imm fork R, into Clumber Park (no charge for cycles), at first × rds, turn R to:	Church (up lane on L), one of smallest in country; Sundial. Belfry, Norman door. National Trust.
1¼	**Clumber Bridge.** Cross bridge and fork L (see note b) through South Park; in 1½m, turn L on track; after passing barrier, cont str ahead, desc to ford, cont through:	Views. Track is rideable. Ford is Uneven, rec to cross by footbridge.

2½	**Hardwick Village.** Turn L and imm after passing head of lake, turn L on track, cont for ¾m and on joining surfaced drive, turn L, cont past Cycle Hire Centre and turn L to:	Estate village. Track is rideable.
1½	**Clumber Park Visitors Centre.** C. On leaving centre, turn R (see note c) and cont past Cricket Ground to × rds; turn R along Lime Tree Avenue (see note d); at next × rds turn L to:	Clumber House demolished in 1938, was formerly the seat of Dukes of Newcastle. Beautiful location. Lake, birds. Lime Tree Avenue is 3¾ miles long. A public road runs through it from Carburton gate to Apley Head Lodge on A614.
2¼	**Manton Lodge.** Imm turn L on byroad and in 150 yds turn R (see e); cont through forest and past Worksop College (on L); at T junc, turn R to TR and cont str ahead, desc to T junc; turn L past Priory Gatehouse and cont along Potter St into:	It is not advisable to emerge on busy main road.
3¾	**WORKSOP**	

Notes
(a) The bridleway section through Welbeck Park can be omitted by continuing along the A60.
(b) The detour around South Park and Hardwick village, can be omitted by retracing route from bridge then keeping R at all junctions direct to Clumber Park Visitors Centre but this omits some pleasant cycling byways (see map).
(c) There is an alternative route by turning L on leaving the Visitors Centre and joining Lime Tree Avenue a short distance to the W (see map).
(d) A more direct route back to Worksop can be taken by continuing straight ahead at × rds to Truman's Lodge and then continuing via the B6005 (see map).
(e) From Manton Lodge, there is an alternative route by keeping L and continuing to Truman's Lodge and then continuing as (c) (see map).

Ride No. 7   CARLTON-IN-LINDRICK and BLYTH   33¾ miles / 54.0 kms

Start: Worksop (Victoria Square)

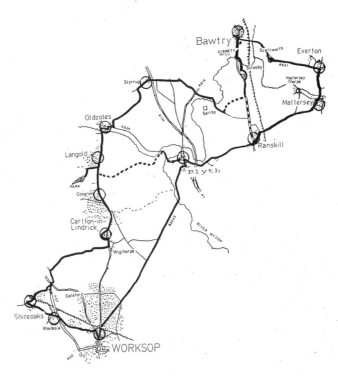

In the northern tip of the county, along the boundary with South Yorkshire, is a web of quiet byroads. Although the route passes close to several collieries, it also leads to some quiet corners notably at Carlton-in-Lindrick, Langold Park, Serlby and Scrooby.

Gradients: Gently undulating terrain ensuring very easy cycling.

Miles	Places, Information and Itinerary	Points of interest and attractions
	WORKSOP. *EC: Thurs, MD: Sat. BR. Sh. C. Cyc.* Take Gateford Road for 200 yds and at mini TR, turn L (Sandy Lane, sp Shireoaks) in ½m at T junc, turn L and in ½m imm before new TR, turn R, cont through:	Priory Gatehouse, 14 cent.; Church - Norman; busy town, centre of coal mining area but nevertheless is the 'Gateway to The Dukeries. River Ryton. Former Chesterfield Canal on L.

1½	**Rhodesia.** Cont ahead to: .	Do not turn into village.
1	**Shireoaks.** *BR. Sh.* Turn R at church; cont over level ×g and in ¼m turn L into 'abandoned' byroad; cont into cul-de-sac; dismount then turn L on A57 (Worksop by-pass); cont to TR and take 2nd exit (sp Woodsetts); in ¼m turn R (sp Carlton Lindrick) and cont through open country for 1¾m, at T junc (A60) turn L into:	Old Mill on L. Former byroad closed when Worksop by-pass was constructed but can still be used by cyclists. Bypass busy, care required.
3¾	**Carlton-in-Lindrick.** *Sh.* Turn L (Church Lane) past Mill and church; cont to T junc (A60), turn L and cont ahead to:	Mill. Church. Carlton Cycles (now part of Raleigh Industries) took its name from the village where the cycles were first made in a blacksmiths shop.
1½	**Cosgrove.** Cont ahead on A60 and imm on entering LANGOLD, turn L (Ramsden Av) imm turn L (Church Lane sp Langold Lake), cont into:	Site of former colliery now an industrial estate.
1	**Langold Park.** Retrace route to junc A60 and turn L through:	C - Limited days/hours. Places to picnic.
¾	**Langold.** Cont ahead (see note a) and cont to:	*Sh.* Built to house employees at local colliery now closed.
1	**Oldcotes.** C. Imm after B6463 junc (on L) turn R (care needed) (Main Road), cont thro village to T junc (A634), turn R and in 200 yds turn L (sp Styrrup) cont through open country to:	Pleasant village street away from main roads.
2	**Styrrup.** Cont thro village and turn R (sp Serlby), cross A1 Motorway and in further ½m at × rds, cont str ahead; in ¼m at T junc, turn R; cont to × rds (A614) and cont str ahead (care needed, busy road); into:	Here was once a Tournament Ground (c1194) but nothing now remains.

2½	**Serlby Park.** Cont through park and on leaving: turn L on track (see note b); cont to T junc (A638); turn L and in ½m on LH bend, turn R (Low Road) into:	Hall in pct woodland setting once seat of Viscount Galway. River Ryton on R. Track is very sandy in middle section, riding very difficult. A638 formerly Great North Road but now much quieter since A1(M) constructed.
1¾	**Scrooby.** Cont thro village and imm after LH bend, turn R past Mill, cont ahead and cross River Ryton; (see note c); cont to × rds at:	William Brewster, one of Pilgrim Fathers lived here in cottage now demolished. Village now much visited by American tourists. Monks Mill, pict.
½	**Gibbet Hill.** Turn R to TR and cont to outskirts of:	Scene of hanging in 1779 at the scene of a murder.
1	**Bawtry.** Sh. C. At TL turn R on A631 (sp Gainsborough), cross bridge (River Idle, county boundary) and in 1m (opp layby) turn R (care required) into:	County boundary is crossed into South Yorkshire as village is entered. See first house on R No. 1 Yorkshire.
1½	**Scaftworth.** Cont through village and at T junc A631 turn R and cont to:	Quiet village bypassed by A631.
2	**Everton.** B&B. Sh C. At × rds turn R and after short climb, desc and cont to:	Cafe is ¼m further along A631.
1¼	**Mattersey.** Cont ahead on B6045 and after crossing main east coast rly line, bear L into:	Ruins of Priory along rough lane to L. River Idle.
2½	**Ranskill.** PM. Sh. In centre of village, turn L and imm turn R (sp B6045 Blyth); cont through open country and at T junc (A634), turn R into:	Old Great North Road is crossed here.
2¼	**Blyth.** Sh. C. Turn L in centre of village and in 250 yds, turn R (sp B6045 Worksop) in 1m cross br (River Ryton) and cont on undulating road; at TL cont str ahead into:	Priory Church, Georgian houses. Base for cycling time trials for many years. Village greens. Once a staging post for coaches on the old highway London-York. River Ryton.

6   WORKSOP

Notes

(a) On the R between Costhorpe and Langold, a bridleway all rideable provides a direct route to Blyth (see map).

(b) On leaving Serlby Park, to avoid the sandy track, continue ahead and turn L on A638. There is a direct route to Ranskill by continuing str ahead on leaving Serlby Park and at T junc (A638), turning R (see map).

(c) The distance may be shortened by turning back from Scrooby direct to Ranskill (see map).

The Monks Mill at Scrooby in the north of the county.

Ride No. 8   WISETON, LITTLEBOROUGH and LANEHAM   37¼ miles / 59.5 kms

Start: East Retford (Market Place)

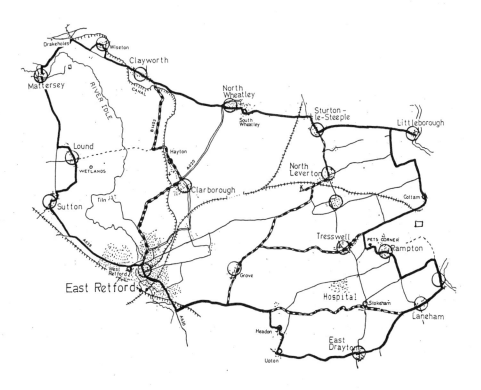

This ride keeps mainly to rural by-roads through the farming area to the north and east of Retford and links together some quiet villages and interesting corners.

Gradients: Very easy with no really steep hills.

Miles	Places, Information and Itinerary	Points of interest and scenic attractions
	EAST RETFORD. *EC:* Wed, *MD:* Sat. Sh. C. Leave by Bridge Street following line of old Great North Road; pass through:	Church - stained glass; Cannon outside church. Impressive market square; River Idle; Chesterfield Canal.

¼	**West Retford.** At TR, cont str ahead (A638); in 1½m at × rds, turn R to:	Hall - Queen Anne period. Church - 14c, tower and spire.
2¾	**Sutton.** Cont thro village and turn R opp church, cont on by-road to:	Wetlands Waterfowl Reserve is along the lane on R. Open daily.
1¼	**Lound.** At × rds cont str ahead to T junc; turn R and cont to:	A quiet village whose cottages cluster round × rds at end of Chain Bridge Lane, a rough track leading to Hayton and Clarborough.
2⅛	**Mattersey.** Turn L at church and imm turn R to footbridge (River Idle); cont on old road and at T junc, turn R B6045 and cont to:	Pleasant village. Ruins of Priory along rough lane to R at church.
1¼	**Drakeholes.** Take first turn R on byroad; in ¾m turn L to:	A road junc where Chesterfield Canal passes through a tunnel, narrow boats. Cafe ½m W off A631.
1	**Wiseton.** Turn R and cont alongside canal, at T junc turn L to:	Hall now demolished. Unspoiled picturesque village.
1¼	**Clayworth.** Cont thro village and then fork L (see note a); climb Haughgate Hill then desc to × rds (A620 North Wheatley Bypass); cont str ahead thro:	A pleasant village with some picturesque cottages lining the street; Chesterfield Canal.
2¾	**North Wheatley.** Turn R then L following line of Roman Road to:	Old houses. Church at South Wheatley, (now abandoned).
1¾	**Sturton-le-Steeple.** Turn R and in ¼m at church, turn L, (see note b); cont to:	Church; a quiet village, of farms and cottages.

3	**Littleborough.** Cont to bank of River Trent then retrace route for ¾m and turn L; cont thro Cotes to:	Now forgotten hamlet but once an important crossing of the Trent by Ermine Street, a Roman road. The former ferry has long since been discontinued. Church. The Aegir* can be seen on the river here.
3½	**Cottam.** Cont past Power Station and in 1½ turn L (see note c); in ½m, turn L past entrance to Pets' Corner, cont to:	The village is overshadowed by the cooling towers of Cottam Power Station, one of several along this stretch of the River Trent. Pets' Corner: Adventure Playground and Tea Gardens, excellent halt for children.
2¾	**Rampton.** *PM*. Cont thro village and in ½m turn L on byroad; in 1m turn R and cont alongside River Trent to:	
2½	**Church Laneham.** Cont through:	River Trent, tidal. Popular for water sports. Church - 11c doorway; oak chests.
1	**Laneham.** *PM*. Cont str ahead and in ½m fork L (see note d) to:	
2½	**East Drayton.** At church, cont str ahead to:	
2¼	**Upton.** Turn R and in ½m turn L through:	
½	**Headon.** In ½m bear L, cont for 2½m, at level × g, cont to T junc; turn R (A638) into:	Byroad on R leads (¾m) to Grove (Cafe at Garden Centre).
4¾	**RETFORD**	

Notes
(a) For a shorter ride, fork R on leaving Clayworth and continue to Hayton, then at × rds on outskirts of Clarborough, turn R on byroad (see map).
(b) From Sturton-le-Steeple, there is an alternative and shorter route via North Leverton which allows a visit to a working windmill and to Grove but this would omit Littleborough and Laneham (see map).

*Aegir is a bore or huge wave which rushes up the river during spring tides

(c) From Cottam, there is an alternative and shorter route via Tresswell and Grove but this would omit Laneham (see map).

(d) ¾m after Laneham, the road to the right is a more direct route to Retford via Stokeham (see map).

The church at Littleborough, one of the smallest in the county, is on the banks of the River Trent and can be visited on Ride No. 8.

Ride No. 9   BOTHAMSALL, TUXFORD and LAXTON   29¾ miles / 47.5 kms

Start: East Retford (Market Place)

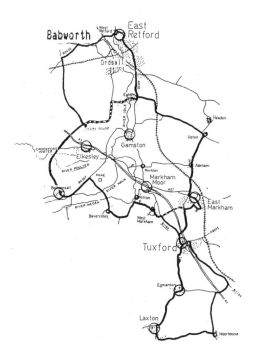

This is a varied route to the south of East Retford, first following the line of the Old Great North Road then, after crossing the new A1, following an off highway route to Bothamsall. There are then more quiet byways to Tuxford and Laxton before returning through East Markham.

Gradients: Generally very easy; a few short climbs in the vicinity of Tuxford.

Miles	Places, Information and Itinerary	Points of interest and scenic attractions
	EAST RETFORD. *EC:* Wed, *MD:* Sat. Sh. C. Leave by Bridge Street following line of old Great North Road:	Church - stained glass; Cannon outside church. Impressive market square; River Idle; Chesterfield Canal.

¼	**West Retford.** At church, turn L and cont to T junc; turn L (A620), cont over rly bridge and cont to:	Hall - Queen Anne period. Church - 14c, tower and spire. Main East Coast line.
1¼	**Babworth,** Turn L (B6420) and cont to road junc, turn L through trees, cross level × g and cont to:	Small village and estate. Site of former Rushy Inn on former Old Great North Road. This byroad was formerly the line of the Old Great North Road.
2½	**Jockey House.** Turn R and cont to junc A1 (dual carriageway); cross str over (very busy road, extreme care when crossing, advisable to dismount); cont on byroad to:	Formerly Inn in the days of stage coaches. See milestone at opposite corner.
1¼	**Crookford Water.** Ford. Cont ahead through forest on track then join surfaced byroad and cont to:	River Poulter, ford very uneven, advisable to cross by footbridge.
1¼	**Bothamsall.** *Sh.* Fork L and after short desc, cont to T junc (B6387); turn L and in 1m turn R and continue past entrance to:	Pict cottages line village street which leads to Castle Hill.
2	**Bevercotes Colliery.** Turn R, cross br (River Meden) then cont to:	Bevercotes, one of Britain's most modern collieries.
½	**Bevercotes.** At T junc turn L; in ½m bear L and cont to:	Small farming hamlet.
1¼	**Milton.** Turn R and after short climb cont to:	Church now abandoned. Contains mausoleum of Duke of Newcastle.

¾	**West Markham.** Turn L at church then R and climb to × rds at junc B1164 (old Great North Road), turn R (see note a) and cont to:	Church, once abandoned now in use again.
1½	**Tuxford.** *EC: Wed, Sh. C.* In Market Square, turn R (Newcastle St) (see note b) cont on undulating road to:	Church - font cover 1673. Old Grammar School. Formerly busy place on Great North Road, now quiet.
1½	**Egmanton.** Fork R through village then fork L and and cont to:	Small peaceful village of farms cottages.
1¼	**Laxton.** *B&B. PM. Sh.* Turn L past Behive Inn and after short desc, fork L on byroad, cont to:	Medieval Crop rotation system still followed. Exhibition at rear Beehive Inn. Church -monuments. Site of Motte & Bailey Castle.
1¾	**Moorhouse.** Turn L and in 1¼m at T junc, turn R, cross br (A1) and at T junc, turn L (B1164) (old Great North Road); cont past A1 link to T junc (A6075); turn L into:	
4	**Tuxford.** At Market Place, turn R and after short desc, turn R (sp East Markham) climb and at × rds, turn R, in ¼m again turn R, cont past church and along main street of:	See above.
2½	**East Markham.** *EC: Wed. Sh.* At × rds turn R, cross over A57 (East Markham Bypass) and cont to:	Church - brass 1419. Fine tower.
1¼	**Askham.** Cont ahead to:	
1	**Upton.** Turn L and after an easy climb desc and cont to T junc (A638) at:	

2¾ **Eaton.** Turn R and cont into:

2¼ **EAST RETFORD.**

Notes
(a) Ride may be shortened by omitting Tuxford and Laxton and riding direct from West Markham to East Markham (see map).
(b) Ride may also be shortened by retracing route from Tuxford and omitting Laxton (see map).

After cycling along the Old Great North Road, long since abandoned by traffic on the A1, the author approaches the Jockey House which was an Inn in the days of stage coaches.

Ride No. 10   SOUTHWELL, OXTON   32 miles/51.0 kms
                   and FISKERTON

Start: Newark-upon-Trent (Castlegate)

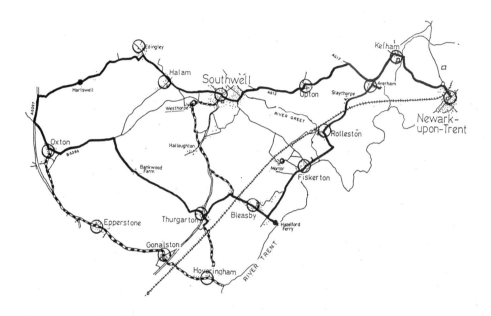

Delightful old world Southwell with its fine cathedral is the first objective on this ride. The return is made by a series of byroads and allows for a visit to Trentside at Hazelford Ferry and Fiskerton.

Gradients: Very easy. The only major climbs are after Hartswell and on the B6386 after leaving Oxton.

Miles	Places, Information and Itinerary	Points of interest and scenic attractions
	NEWARK-UPON-TRENT. *Inf.* BR. B&B. Sh. C. Cyc. From Castlegate, Turn L and cross br (River Devon) then level ×g, cont to new TR and take 2nd exit (sp A617 Mansfield); cont for 1½m then cross br (River Trent) into:	Castle (ruins) 12c-15c. King John died here. Junction of Fosse Way and Great North Road. Church - fine spire. Impressive market place. Old houses. Beaumond Cross. Gladstone was once town's MP.

Thurgarton is a delightful village with some pleasant corners. A stream flows alongside the byroad to Hoveringham.

1¾	**Kelham.** *PM.* Cont str thro village to outskirts of:	Hall now District Council offices formerly a Religious House. Church - Lexington monuments. River Trent.
1	**Averham.** Cont on A617 and in further ¾m fork L (A612) cont to:	Small Trentside village with Theatre and Church.
1¼	**Upton.** *Sh.* Cont through village and in 2 miles, cross br (River Greet); cont into:	Quiet village.
3½	**SOUTHWELL.** *EC: Thurs, MD: Sat. B&B. Sh. PM. C.* At T junc turn R (see note a) and imm turn L on narrow street, cont ahead for 1m then after short climb, desc into:	Cathedral - Norman and later. Archbishop's Palace ruins. Saracens Head Inn - assoc with Charles I. Burgage Manor - assoc Lord Byron. Once a Youth Hostel. Merryweather's Nursery. Birthplace of Bramley Apple. River Greet.
2	**Halam.** Cont through village and climb easily for 1m then turn L into narrow byroad; cont through:	Church; quiet village, most of cottages along side byroads.
4	**Hartswell.** Climb for ½m then desc to T junc (A6097) busy road; turn L and in ¾m at × rds turn L (sp Oxton); desc into:	Quiet narrow byroad through straggling hamlet.
2½	**Oxton.** *PM. Sh.* Turn L and in ½m at T junc, turn L (see note b) climb steeply for ½m; in further ¾m, turn R (sp Bridleway, Bankwood Farm); cont past farm and through open country, desc to T junc and cont to:	Parkland setting. Church: citation for VC awarded to Capt (later Rear Admiral) R St. V. Sherbrook, commander of HMS Onslow at battle of North Cape, Dec. 1942. Surface of bridleway good.
5¼	**Thurgarton.** *EC: Tues. Sh.* At × rds (junc A612) cont ahead to:	Castle Hill. Boots Experimental Fruit Farm. Priory Church.

¾	**Goverton.** Turn R and cross level ×g into:	
¾	**Bleasby.** *PM. C.* Cont str ahead thro village and at × rds, cont ahead to:	Wagon & Horses Inn - attractive. Cafe popular with cyclists.
1	**Hazelford Ferry.** Retrace route to × rds; turn R and cont to:	River Trent, popular stretch. Ferry now discontinued.
2	**Fiskerton.** *PM.* Cont str ahead alongside river to:	Pleasant riverside village.
1½	**Rolleston.** Turn R and cont through Staythorpe to:	Southwell Racecourse along lane to L.
1¾	**Averham.** At T junc (A617), turn R and retrace outward route through:	Church. Theatre.
1	**Kelham** and cont to:	
2	**NEWARK-UPON-TRENT.**	

Notes

(a) The ride may be shortened by turning left in SOUTHWELL and riding direct via Westhorpe to Bleasby (see map).

(b) From Oxton, there is an alternative route via Epperstone and Gonalston with an extension to Hoveringham (C) joining the main route at Thurgarton (see map).

Ride No. 11 KIRKLINGTON and LAXTON 35½ miles / 57.0 kms

Start: Newark (Castlegate)

Although there are no special highlights on this ride, it is a very pleasant route which wanders through secluded byroads in the heart of the county.

Gradients: For the most part, the route is gently undulating with only occasional climbs, the steepest being after leaving Kirklington.

Miles	*Places, Information and Itinerary*	*Points of interest and scenic attractions*
	NEWARK-UPON-TRENT. *Inf.* BR. B&B. Sh. C. Cyc. · From Castlegate turn L and cross br (River Devon) and level × g then cont to new TR; take 3rd exit and follow line of old Great North Road crossing River Trent by South Muskham Bridge to TR at:	Castle (ruins) 12c-15c. King John died here. Junction of Fosse Way and Great North Road. Church - fine spire. Impressive market place. Old houses. Beaumond Cross. Gladstone was once town's MP. TR on new bypass opened 1989; (former Southwell Road now closed). Works of British Sugar Corporation on R.

On Ride No. 11, the author diverted into the lovely village of Caunton and paused by the Beck where it flows past the church.

2	**South Muskham.** Take 3rd exit (see note a) and in 300 yds, turn L (sp Bathley, Crow Lane); At T junc turn R to:	Pleasant village hidden away along quiet byroads (see diversion in note a).
1¾	**Bathley.** PM. Cont thro village to × rds, cont str ahead (sp Norwell), at next × rds, turn L; climb for ½m then desc and cont into:	Small quiet hamlet, pleasant country byroads.
2¾	**Norwell.** PM. At T junc turn R and in ¼m turn L (sp Ossington); in 50 yds again turn L (sp Ossington); cont thro open country; in 2m at T junc turn L to:	Small village at junc of several byroads.
3½	**Ossington.** Turn R (sp Moorhouse) (see note b) and cont to:	Former country estate; house now demolished; church along lane to R.
1½	**Moorhouse.** Fork L to:	
2¼	**Laxton.** B&B. PM. Sh. T. Retrace route for ¼m then fork R (sp Kneesall); cont to × rds and turn R (sp Kneesall) (see note c); on approach to:	Medieval crop rotation system still followed. Exhibition at rear of Beehive Inn. Church - monuments. Site of Motte & Bailey Castle.
2¼	**Kneesall.** Turn L into narrow byroad (School Lane) and cont to junc A616; turn R past chuch and in 200 yds turn L (sp Eakring); in 1½m turn R and cont into:	Quiet village on A616 Newark-Ollerton road.
2¾	**Eakring.** Turn L (sp Kirklington) (see note d); climb for ¼m then desc to T junc (A617); turn L to:	Church - Norman, assoc with Rev Wm Mompesson who moved here after the Plague at Eyam (Derbys); monument at spot where he preached in field to SW of village.

3¼	**Kirklington.** Sh. Cont on A617 and climb steeply for ¼m; in 1m turn L (sp Winkburn) and cont into:	Straggling village on A617 Mansfield-Newark road.
3	**Winkburn.** Turn L in village and cont to:	Pict estate village, quiet. River Wink.
1¾	**Maplebeck.** *PM*. Turn R and in ¼m at T junc, again turn R; cont to T junc (A616); turn R and in 200 yds turn L into:	Another peaceful secluded village in agricultural area.
2½	**Caunton.** Turn R and cont to × rds (junc A616); turn L and in 1m turn R into byroad (sp Averham) (care needed); in further 1m turn L and cont on undulating byroad to:	Church; Windmill. Ford across The Beck. Birthplace of Dean Hole.
4¼	**Kelham.** At junc A617, turn L through village, cross br (River Trent); cont for 1¾m to TR; take 2nd exit and cont into:	Hall now offices of local District Council was formerly a religious house; Church, Lexington monuments; River Trent.

NEWARK-UPON-TRENT.

Notes

(a) By turning R (4th exit), there is an alternative route through South and North Muskham (Trent riverside) which rejoins the above route to the North of Bathley (see map).

(b) By continuing straight ahead at Ossington, there is a direct route to Kneesall but this omits Laxton (see map).

(c) From the × rds, 1½m beyond Laxton, there is a direct route through Kersall to Maplebeck (see map).

(d) By retracing route from Eakring then forking Right, there is a direct route to Maplebeck (see map).

Ride No. 12   **ASLOCKTON and**   **30 miles/48.0 kms**
                    FLINTHAM

Start: Newark-upon-Trent (Beaumond Cross)

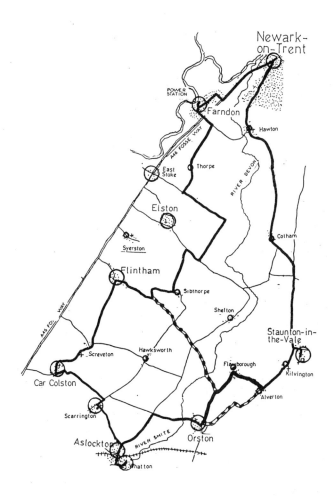

This ride is through a network of byways on either side of the Rivers Devon and Smite to the south of Newark-upon-Trent between the busy A1 and A46 Fosse Roads. It passes through pastoral countryside and many quiet peaceful villages and is an ideal ride for a holiday weekend when main roads are crowded with motor traffic rushing towards the coast.

Gradients: Very easy with no hills.

Miles	Places, Information and Itinerary	Points of interest and scenic attractions
	NEWARK-UPON-TRENT From the TL at Beaumond Cross, turn S along Albert Road; in ½m at TR cont str ahead to:	Castle (ruins) 12c-15c. King John died here. Junction of Fosse Way and Great North Road. Church - fine spire. Impressive market place. Old houses. Beaumond Cross. Gladstone was once town's MP.
1½	**Hawton.** Cont ahead through:	Mentioned in Doomsday Book; Church: 14c, Easter sepulchre.
2½	**Cotham.** Cont ahead for ¾m and at T junc, turn R (sp Staunton) and cont for 2¾m then turn L into:	Small village of farms and cottages.
3	**Staunton-in-the-Vale.** *PM.* Turn R to Church; retrace route and then turn L (sp Orston) through:	Beautiful location near to county boundary with Leicestershire; Church and Hall hidden away in cul-de-sac; Staunton family tombs.
1	**Kilvington.** Cont ahead to outskirts of:	
½	**Alverton** and turn R (sp Flawborough) (see note a); through:	
1	**Flawborough.** In ½m turn L (sp Orston) (see note b) to:	Small village tucked away along quiet byroad.
1½	**Orston.** Turn R through village, cross br (River Smite) and at × rds, turn L (sp Aslockton) (see note c); cont into:	Pict cottages grouped around church and Inn.
2¼	**Aslockton.** Cont through village and at T junc, turn L and in 250 yds, again turn L into:	River Smite. Birthplace of Archbishop Cranmer.

½	**Whatton.** Ride through backroads of village then retrace route to and thro:	Diversion around backroads of village recommended; picturesque cottages.
½	**Aslockton.** Turn L (sp Scarrington) to:	
1¼	**Scarrington.** Imm past church turn R (sp Hawkesworth) and in ¼m turn L (sp Car Colston); to:	Horshoes piled at side of smithy. Quiet village.
1¾	**Car Colston.** Turn R (sp Screveton); cont past church to:	Peaceful village with large green and cricket field. Church: 14c, Chancel. Hall: 17c.
1	**Screveton.** Cont thro village and then fork L to:	Church: Whaley tomb, font.
1½	**Flintham.** Turn R and in ¾m turn L (sp Sibthorpe) to:	Small village set back from A46 Fosse Way.
1¾	**Sibthorpe.** Turn L (sp Elston); in 1m turn R (sp Shelton) and in ½m turn L (sp Thorpe); in 1m turn L and in further 1m turn R (sp Thorpe); cont through:	Birthplace of Archbishop Secker. Church: Easter sepluchre. (Lane to L leads (½) to Elston, once home of Erasmus and Charles Darwin).
4	**Thorpe.** In 1m at T junc turn L to × rds at junc A46 (busy main road); cont str ahead into:	
2	**Farndon.** PM. C. Sh. T. Cont to riverside (River Trent); retrace route then turn L (Wyke Lane); in 200 yds turn L (Marsh Lane) then turn R (Long Lane); at T junc (A46), turn L and return to:	Pleasant riverside rather spoiled by view of Averham Power Station on opposite bank.
2½	**NEWARK-UPON-TRENT.**	

Notes
(a) There is an alternative route to Orston by continuing straight ahead through Alverston village (see map).
(b) The distance may be shortened by turning R half-mile beyond Flawborough and riding direct to Sibthorpe although this omits several interesting villages (see map).
(c) Aslockton and Whatton may be omitted by continuing straight ahead and taking a direct route to Scarrington (see map).

CYCLING NOTES